T0195961

My children, Elizabeth (a doctor) and Tonito (an attorney) inspired me to write this book to help parents and grandparents with small children during these difficult pandemic times safely at home. I hope small children will like it and enjoy the zoo animals.

WELCOME

Little One

elephant

"Mommy, the peacock is calling you. He is loud," said Tonito.

"Feed him, sweetie," said Mommy.

"Look Mommy, the peacock is eating the cat's food again," said Tonito, smiling.

"He is so smart Tonito," said Mommy.

"He drank water from the hanging hose again," said Tonito as the peacock leaves the front door.

"He is saying goodbye with his tail," said Tonito.

"Where did you learn this Tonito?" said Mommy, with a hard-to-believe look on her face.

"From the peacock," said Tonito, running to his room.

"Who did you learn peacock language from honey?" said Mommy, laughing.

Tonito rolled under the bed, laughing. "From the T.V. Mommy," said Tonito.

"WOW! Elephants are huge, Mommy," said Tonito.

"They are the largest remaining land animals. They have a long trunk, tusks, big ear flaps and huge legs," said Mommy.

"What is a trunk?" asked Tonito. "It is the union of an elephant's upper lip and nose. The trunk is used for breathing, bringing food and water to the mouth and grabbing objects.

Trunks can lift up to 800 pounds. They also work as weapons and as tools for moving objects," said Mommy.

"COOL! I want one," said Tonito, laughing. "What about the babies?"

"Sweetie, their babies rely on their mothers for as long as three years," said Mommy.

"How long do they live?" asked Tonito.

"Up to 70 years in the wild," said Mommy.

"They are big like an elephant Mommy," said Tonito.

"Not quite honey. They are a semiaquatic mammal," said Mommy.

"WHAT?" said Tonito, laughing.

"It means living partly on land and partly in water. Adults weigh about 3,300 pounds," said Mommy.

"Are they fast Mommy?" said Tonito.

"Yes baby. They can run 20 miles per hour over short distances. During the day, they remain cool by staying in the water or mud. They have the babies in the water."

"Yuck!" said Tonito.

"The hippo is among the most threatening animal in the world. They are very aggressive and unpredictable," said Mommy.

"Mommy, why do giraffes have such long necks?" asked Tonito.

"Honey, because they like to eat the leaves on tree tops. They also use the necks as weapons in combat," said Mommy.

"As weapons, how?" asked Tonito.

"They use it to fight other males, just as a male antelope uses its horns to fight," said Mommy.

"Do they live long?" asked Tonito.

"About 38 years, Sweetie," said Mommy.

TONITO FEEDING THE GIRAFFE

"How do they sleep?" asked Tonito.
"By lying with its body on top of its folded legs," responded Mommy.

"Glad I am not a giraffe," said Tonito, laughing.

"Look at that Panda," said Tonito.
"Looks like the teddy bear you had as a baby," responded Mommy.

"Where do they come from?" asked Tonito.

"Panda bears are native to south central China. They have large, black spots around the eyes, over the ears, and across their round body," said Mommy.

LET'S HUG!

"What do they eat Mommy?" asked Tonito.
"They love bamboo shoots and leaves and they make up more than 90% of their diet," said Mommy.

"How big are they?" asked Tonito.
"Adults measure around 4 to 6 feet long, including a tail of about 6 inches. Males can weigh up to 350 pounds. The panda's paw has a thumb and five fingers," said Mommy.

"How long do they live?" asked Tonito.

"They live around 20 years in the wild and 30 years in captivity. A female named Jia Jia was the oldest panda ever in captivity. She lived 38 years before she died," explained Mommy.

"Look at the big orange monkey, Mommy," said Tonito.

Mommy smiles. "It is called an orangutan, baby, and they are among the most intelligent primates. The orange-reddish brown colored hair is a result of sunlight reflecting off the hair," said Mommy.

"What long arms he has," said Tonito.

"They have a large, bulky body, a thick neck, very long strong arms, short, bowed legs and no tail," said Mommy.

"What a big head he has," said Tonito.

"He sure does baby," said Mommy.

"Look at those hands," said Tonito.

"They are similar to human hands. They have four long fingers, but a shorter opposable thumb for strong branch gripping as they travel high in the trees. They are not true knuckle-walkers, but are instead fist-walkers," said Mommy.

"What do they eat?" asked Tonito.

"Fruits make up 65-90% of their diet. Most of the day is spent feeding, resting, and traveling.

They also can't swim," said Mommy.

"Are the zebra lines black or white?" asked Tonito.

"Zebras are black with white stripes Sweetie," said Mommy.

"Are they fast like horses?" asked Tonito.

"Yes. Their top speed is about 40 miles per hour," said Mommy.

"Did you know they stand up while sleeping and they have never been truly tamed," said Mommy.

"No way," responded Tonito.

"Yes, way. Zebras can weigh about 800 pounds," said Mommy.

"Just about like me," said Tonito, laughing.

"Yes, right," she said, smiling.

"Tiger babies are funny," said Tonito.

"Yes, they are, Honey. They stay with the mother for about 2 years," said Mommy.

"They are strong," said Tonito.

"Yes. Tigers have a powerful body with strong forelimbs. They are also strong swimmers. They like to bathe in ponds, lakes and rivers," said Mommy.

"They have big teeth," said Tonito.

"Yes, and the tail is about half the length of its body and they normally weigh about 700 pounds," said Mommy. "That is a lot," said Tonito.

"Yes, baby. They normally live to be around 8 years. The oldest recorded caged tiger lived for 26 years," said Mommy.

"Tell me about lions, Mommy," asked Tonito.

"They are muscular with a short, rounded head and a short neck and round ears," responded Mommy.

"How much do they weigh?" asked Tonito.

"Males weigh about 500 pounds and females about 350 pounds. Lions spend much of their time resting, about 20 hours per day," said Mommy.

"What else?" asked Tonito.

"About 2 hours a day they spend walking and 50 minutes eating," said Mommy.

"Gorillas live in the forests of Africa. They are the largest living primates," said Mommy.

"They walk funny," said Tonito. "They move around by knuckle-walking," said Mommy.

"They are so big," said Tonito. "Wild male gorillas weigh about 400 pounds while females weigh about 250 pounds. Males are about 6 feet tall and females are about 5 feet tall," said Mommy.

"What do they eat?" asked Tonito. "Leaves, stems and fruits. They rarely drink water," said Mommy. "No water? No way," said Tonito.

"No water. Because the vegetables they eat are full of water. Also, they live in groups called troops and the silver back is the center of attention. He is the boss," said Mommy.

"Are they smart?" asked Tonito. "Highly intelligent like you Sweetie," they both, smile.

About the Author

Tony Mesa, Jr., was born in Havana, Cuba. At age 15 he emigrated to the United States, having to flee the communist dictatorship without his parents. Upon graduating college, he worked as an executive for several, multinational corporations before dedicating nearly half his career to the non-profit sector where he served as Senior Vice President and Chief Financial Officer. He is now retired and resides in Miami, Florida with his wife Carrie of 52 years. "Welcome to the Zoo" was born of a desire to help parents engage and entertain small children during the global pandemic and allow them to explore a zoo and learn about wild animals all while sheltering safely at home during the crisis.

About Elizabeth

Dr. Elizabeth D. Mesa completed her undergraduate studies in psychology at Florida International University and continued in her graduate studies at Nova Southeastern University, obtaining a Master's degree in Mental Health Counseling and a Doctoral degree in Clinical Psychology. She loves zoo animals.

Dr. Mesa has worked in a variety of clinical settings and is a clinical psychologist at a hospital in Florida.

About Tonito

"Tonito" is Dr. Mesa's younger brother. As a child he loved going to the zoo and visiting Walt Disney World with his family.

Color Me!

Tony Mesa, Jr.
Author

Archway Publishing books may be ordered through booksellers or by contacting:

Archway Publishing
1663 Liberty Drive
Bloomington, IN 47403
www.archwaypublishing.com
1 (888) 242-5904

ISBN: 978-1-4808-9360-3 (sc)
ISBN: 978-1-4808-9361-0 (hc)
ISBN: 978-1-4808-9359-7 (e)

Print information available on the last page.

Archway Publishing rev. date: 08/13/2020

Printed in the United States
By Bookmasters

Tonito loves learning about all the animals who live at the zoo.

Guided by wisdom from his mommy, Tonito discovers fun facts and the interesting characteristics of peacocks, elephants, hippos, giraffes, pandas, orange monkeys, and so many more!

In this colorful children's book, a little boy learns all about zoo animals, their special strengths and talents, and how they interact with the world around them.

ARCHWAY
PUBLISHING

U.S. $16.95

ISBN 978-1-4808-9360-3

5169

9 781480 893603

A Nasty Virus has Struck the World,
so the Giraffes Stay Home to Stay Safe

Written by Julie Sorenson   ●   Illustrated by Richelle Bower